Sing a Song of Opposites

by Pam Schiller

 Wright Group

The text from this book can be sung using the tune to "Mary Had a Little Lamb."

Photo Credits:
Cover, (t) ©Renee Lynn/CORBIS-Stock Market, (b) ©Tui De Roy/Minden Pictures; **3,** ©SuperStock; **4-5,** ©Art Wolfe/Stone; **6,** ©Stone; **8,** ©Bob Daemmrich/Stock Boston; **9,** (t) ©Laurance B. Aiuppy/FPG International, (b) ©David Young-Wolff/Stone; **10,** ©Darrell Gulin/Stone; **12,** (t) (b) ©David Young-Wolff/PhotoEdit; **13,** (t) ©FPG International, (b) ©Mary Kate Denny/PhotoEdit; **14-15,** ©Sun Star/Mauritius/H. Armstrong Roberts; **16,** ©Richard Hansen/Photo Researchers, Inc.; **17** (t) (b) ©Michael Newman/PhotoEdit; **18-19,** ©Stone; **20,** (t) ©Fotopic International Camerique Inc., Int'l./H. Armstrong Roberts, (b) ©David Young-Wolff/PhotoEdit; **21** (t) ©CORBIS-Stock Market, (b) ©Richard T. Nowitz/CORBIS; **22,** ©Renee Lynn/CORBIS-Stock Market; **23,** ©Tui De Roy/Minden Pictures.

www.WrightGroup.com

 **Wright Group**

Send all inquiries to:
Wright Group/McGraw-Hill
P.O. Box 812960
Chicago, IL 60681

ISBN 0-07-572407-3

10 QST 09 08 07

This is **big,**

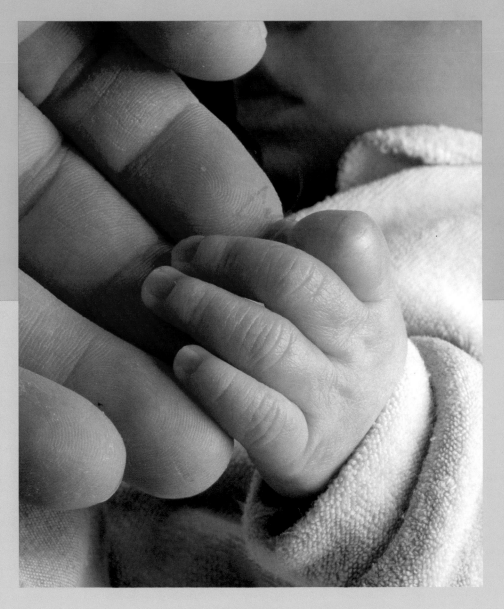

and this is small.

This is **big;**

this is small.

This is **big,**

and this is
small.

Sing along with me.

This is tall,

and this is short.

This is tall;

this
is short.

This is tall,

and this is short.

Sing along with me.

This is up,

and this
is down.

This
is up;

this is down.

This is up,

and this
is down.

Sing along with me.

This is in,

and this is out.

This is in;

this is out.

This is in,

and
this
is out.

Sing along with me.

This is fast,

and this is slow.

This is fast;

this is slow.

This is fast,

and this is slow.

Sing along with me.

The text from this book
can be sung using the tune to
"Mary Had a Little Lamb."

Suggested additional verses:

This is soft, and this is hard.
This is soft; this is hard.
This is soft, and this is hard.
Sing along with me.

This is happy, and this is sad....

This is here, and this is there....

Pam Schiller